Margaret Chase Smith: A Woman for President

A TIME LINE BIOGRAPHY

Lynn Plourde

Illustrated by David McPhail

Charlesbridge

For Margaret Chase Smith:
     what an inspiration she was, and still is.
          —L. P.

For young women everywhere:
     aspire, aspire!
          —D. M.

The time lines in this book highlight key historical events and are not intended to represent chronological scale.

Text copyright © 2008 by Lynn Plourde
Illustrations copyright © 2008 by David McPhail and John O'Connor

Published by Charlesbridge
85 Main Street, Watertown, MA 02472
(617) 926-0329 • www.charlesbridge.com

Library of Congress Cataloging-in-Publication Data
Plourde, Lynn.
   Margaret Chase Smith : a woman for president / Lynn Plourde.
      p. cm.
   ISBN 978-1-58089-234-6 (reinforced for library use)
   ISBN 978-1-58089-235-3 (softcover)
1. Smith, Margaret Chase, 1897–1995—Juvenile literature. 2. Women legislators—United States—Biography—Juvenile literature. 3. Legislators—United States—Biography. 4. United States. Congress. Senate—Biography. 5. Women presidential candidates—United States—Biography—Juvenile literature. 6. Presidential candidates—United States—Biography—Juvenile literature. I. Title.
E748.S667P58 2008
328.73'092—dc22 [B]   2007013549

Printed in the United States of America
(hc) 10 9 8 7 6 5 4 3 2 1
(sc) 10 9 8 7 6 5 4 3 2 1

Illustrations done in pen and ink and watercolor on Arches paper
Text type set in Sabon and display type set in Woodrow by Chank Diesel, Minneapolis
Color separations by Chroma Graphics, Singapore
Printed and bound by Lake Book Manufacturing, Inc.
Production supervision by Brian G. Walker
Designed by Susan Mallory Sherman

She *couldn't* become President of the United States. She was a she! Only a man could be elected president . . . right?

Maybe not.

In 1964 Senator Margaret Chase Smith made an announcement. She began her speech by explaining why she should *not* run for president: she didn't have enough money, most thought there was no chance she could win, plus some people said a woman wouldn't have the energy for a national campaign.

She concluded, "Because of these very impelling reasons *against* my running, I have decided that I *shall*. . . ."

What a president she would have been—a surprising one.

When Margaret Chase Smith was born in 1897 in the small Maine town of Skowhegan, women in most of the United States could not even vote—not for dogcatcher, not for governor, and most certainly not for president. It wasn't until 1920 that women throughout the country could legally cast their ballots.

Margaret came from a poor family. Her father was a barber who drank too much and suffered from severe headaches. Her mother frequently worked outside the home waiting tables and stitching shoes to help support the family. They lived at Margaret's grandfather's house because they could not afford their own home.

What a daughter she was—one who came from humble roots.

The right to vote

★	★	★	★	★
1789	**1870**	**1920**	**1924**	**1961**
First US elections: only white adult men who own property can vote	15th Amendment gives black men the right to vote	19th Amendment gives women the right to vote	Indian Citizenship Act assures Native Americans the right to vote	23rd Amendment gives citizens of Washington DC the right to vote

1965
Voting Rights Act
outlaws literacy test
for voters

1971
26th Amendment
lowers voting age
from 21 to 18

Margaret faced challenges and tragedy early on. When her baby brother Roland suffered from convulsions, she helped to care for him. He died of pneumonia at the age of one. Three years later, Margaret's two-year-old brother Lawrence also died, from dysentery, an infection of the digestive system.

The family could not afford to have a gravestone carved for the brothers, but Margaret's mother ordered one anyway. Then she did laundry and ironing for the stonecutter's family in order to pay for it. Margaret did her share, too. Every day before school—even on cold, snowy mornings—she walked a mile to the stonecutter's house to deliver a quart of fresh milk from her family's cow.

What a sister she was—a compassionate and responsible one.

US life expectancy

1900	1925	1940s	1950	1975	2000
47 years*	59 years	The medicine penicillin comes into widespread use	68 years	73 years	77 years†

* leading causes of death are pneumonia, tuberculosis, and dysentery
† leading causes of death are heart disease, stroke, and cancer

From the time she first learned to speak, Margaret called her grandfather Banker, perhaps because it was easier for her to pronounce than "Grandfather." Whatever the reason, the nickname was most appropriate. Even though Banker worked at a factory, not a bank, he was the most frugal person Margaret knew.

As a senior in high school, Margaret wanted to leave Maine for the first time to go on a class trip to Washington DC. Her parents couldn't afford to send her, but one day Banker brought Margaret to the bank and withdrew sixty dollars to pay for her trip. Then he made Margaret sign a note promising to pay him back every penny of that sixty dollars—plus six percent interest!

What a granddaughter she was—one who learned the value of money.

US incomes*

1900	1910s	1920s	1930s	1940s	1950s	1960s
$12.98/week for 59 hours of work: 22 cents per hour, or $675/year	$750/year	$1,236/year	$1,368/year	$1,299/year	$2,992/year	$4,743/year

figures not adjusted for inflation

1970s $7,564/year   **1980s** $15,757/year   **1999** $534.80/week for 40 hours of work: $13.37 per hour, or $27,810/year

When Margaret graduated from high school, she could not afford to go to college. She tried different jobs, working at a one-room schoolhouse, in a telephone company office, and for a newspaper.

Margaret also became involved in women's organizations, including the Daughters of the American Revolution, Business and Professional Women, and Sorosis, one of the first women's professional clubs in the nation. She soon became a leader in these organizations. Margaret considered these experiences her "college education."

What a student she was—one who learned much from the real world.

US graduation rates

1910	1920	1940	1970
24% of all students attend fewer than 5 years of elementary school	16% of the population graduate from high school, 3% from college	26% of women and 23% of men graduate from high school	55% of both men and women graduate from high school; 14% of men and 8% of women graduate from college

1980
From this point onward, women make up the majority of college students

1990
78% of both men and women graduate from high school

2005
85% of both men and women graduate from high school; 29% of men and 27% of women graduate from college

After graduation, Margaret began dating town selectman and state legislator Clyde Smith, who was twenty-one years older than she was. Even though Margaret and Clyde were both adults, her parents still chaperoned their dates.

In 1930, after more than a decade of courtship, the couple married. Margaret wasn't a traditional wife who knew about cooking and housework, although she did learn to make a New England meal of baked beans and brown bread to serve to Clyde's political guests. Once when Margaret tried to impress Clyde by making fish chowder, he suggested she spend her time "to better advantage."

So she did, helping her husband with his political duties. She kept track of his appointments, took notes at meetings he attended, and drove him all over the state to campaign.

What a wife she was—one who was valued as a political partner.

US women working outside the home

1900	1920	1940	1960	1980	2000
19%	21%	25%	38%	52%	60%

In 1936, Clyde was elected to the U.S. House of Representatives. Margaret loved living in Washington. She called on the First Lady at the White House, joined an organization for congressmen's wives, and took public-speaking lessons. Margaret seemed to be getting ready for bigger and better things.

Before things got better, though, they got worse. Clyde died suddenly, and Margaret became a widow. She was only forty-two years old. She had little time to mourn. It had been Clyde's deathbed wish that Margaret take his place in Congress. One month after Clyde died, Margaret won a special election to finish out his term. It was the first election of many during her eight years in the House of Representatives and her twenty-four years in the Senate.

What a congresswoman she was—ready to serve at a moment's notice.

US women in Congress

1917	1922	1925	1950	1965
Jeannette Rankin of Montana, first woman elected to Congress	Rebecca Latimer Felton of Georgia, first woman to serve in the Senate	3 congresswomen (0 female senators) serve in the 69th Congress	9 congresswomen and 1 female senator (Margaret Chase Smith) serve in the 81st Congress	Patsy Mink of Hawai'i, first Asian American congresswoman

1969
Shirley Chisholm of New York, first African American congresswoman

1975
19 congresswomen (0 senators) serve in the 94th Congress

1989
Ileana Ros-Lehtinen of Florida, first Hispanic congresswoman

1993
Carol Moseley Braun of Illinois, first African American female senator

1999
58 congress-women and 9 female senators serve in the 106th Congress

2007
74 congresswomen and 16 female senators serve in 110th Congress; Nancy Pelosi of California, first female Speaker of the House

Margaret, as a woman in a man's world and a high school graduate among college graduates, was determined to prove she belonged in Congress. She did so with hard work and by paying attention to details. She personally answered thousands of letters, carefully researched issues before congressional hearings, and wrote a newspaper column giving voters an inside view of Congress.

Margaret was sent to the House, and later to the Senate, to vote on the nation's business—and vote she did. For thirteen years, Margaret did not miss a single congressional roll-call vote. She voted a record-breaking 2,941 consecutive times.

What a senator she was—dedicated and hardworking.

Congressional record setters

★ 1797	★ 1960	★ 1968	★ 1973
Congressman William Charles Cole Claiborne of Tennessee, youngest person elected to Congress (22 years old)	Edith Nourse Rogers of Massachusetts, longest-serving congresswoman (1925–1960)	Margaret Chase Smith of Maine, most consecutive roll-call votes in the Senate (2,941 from 1955–1968); record broken in 1988	Margaret Chase Smith of Maine, longest-serving female senator (1949–1973)

Margaret was a strong military supporter. She worked to make certain that the United States would be ready for any crisis or attack. As Margaret began her senate career, she chose Major General Bill Lewis as her administrative assistant. He worked by her side as her personal and political best friend for more than thirty years.

Margaret helped women in the military receive the same status and benefits as men with her landmark legislation, the Women's Armed Services Integration Act. Previously, women were considered volunteers in the military and received no benefits.

As a woman in Congress, Margaret was not expected to be a leader on military issues. But many were learning to expect the unexpected from Margaret.

What a fighter she was—one determined to defend her country.

Women in the US military

1775–1783	1866	1901	1908	1914–1918	1941	1941–1945
In the Revolutionary War, women serve as nurses, cooks, water carriers, laundresses, and saboteurs	Dr. Mary Walker, first and only woman to receive the Medal of Honor	Army Nurse Corps established	Navy Nurse Corps established	Women allowed to serve as yeomen (secretarial Navy officials) during World War I	Annie Fox, first woman to receive the Purple Heart medal	More than 400,000 women serve in non-combat jobs during World War II

1948	1949	1967	1975	1991	1993	2005
Women's Armed Services Integration Act passed	Air Force Nurse Corps established	Women allowed to be promoted to admirals or generals	Women allowed to enter service academies	Women allowed to fly in combat	Women allowed to serve on combat ships	One out of seven Americans serving in the Iraq War is a woman

Margaret was also passionate about flight and space exploration. As a reporter in 1925, she took her first ride in a biplane. Years later, wearing an orange jumpsuit and high heels, Senator Smith rode in an F-100F Super Sabre as it broke the sound barrier.

As a member of the Aeronautical and Space Sciences Committee, Margaret supported space exploration, prompting the head of NASA to say, "If it were not for a woman, Margaret Chase Smith, we would never have placed a man on the moon."

What an adventurer she was—one who reached for the stars.

Flight and space exploration

1903	**1927**	**1932**	**1947**	**1957**	**1961**
Orville and Wilbur Wright, first airplane flight (12 seconds and 120 feet)	Charles Lindbergh, first solo flight across the Atlantic	Amelia Earhart, first woman to fly solo across the Atlantic	Chuck Yeager, first flight to break the speed of sound	Soviet Union launches first man-made satellite (Sputnik I)	Yuri Gagarin, first man in space

1962	1969	1971	1981	1998	2000
John Glenn, first American to orbit the earth	Neil Armstrong and Buzz Aldrin, first men to walk on the moon	Soviet Union launches first space station (Salyut I)	United States launches first reusable space shuttle (Columbia)	International Space Station launches	First crew arrives to live on International Space Station

In the late 1940s something called the Red Scare was sweeping across the United States. Red symbolized communism, a political and economic system that many Americans believed was a threat to freedom. Senator Joseph McCarthy began unjustly accusing many Americans of being communists. Innocent people were losing their friends and their jobs—because of gossip, not because of facts. No one dared to speak up against Senator McCarthy for fear of seeming unpatriotic. No one, that is, except Margaret. In 1950 she gave her now famous "Declaration of Conscience" speech.

> *The right to criticize; the right to hold unpopular beliefs; the right to protest; the right of independent thought. The exercise of these rights should not cost one single American citizen his reputation or his right to a livelihood. . . . Otherwise none of us could call our souls our own.*

What a leader she was—one who dared to speak the truth.

Cold War

1945
YALTA CONFERENCE: leaders of the United States, Great Britain, and the Soviet Union disagree about what should happen to Europe after WWII; **HIROSHIMA AND NAGASAKI:** the US drops an atomic bomb on each of these Japanese cities

1948–1949
BERLIN BLOCKADE: Due to rising tension with the West, the Soviet Union (which controls the area around Berlin) blocks road and rail access to Western-occupied sections of the city for 320 days

1950–1953
KOREAN WAR: the Soviet Union supports communist North Korea while the US supports South Korea

1962
CUBAN MISSILE CRISIS: the US and the Soviet Union come close to nuclear war over the placement of Soviet nuclear missiles in Cuba

It was said that if a man had delivered the "Declaration of Conscience" speech, he would have been the next president. Margaret was not a man, however, and no one was rushing to put her in the White House. Many fellow Republicans still supported Senator McCarthy and treated Margaret as an outcast.

Margaret decided to let the people, not politicians, decide if she should be president. While campaigning in 1964 Margaret listed her qualifications: years of experience, independence, and a determination to take "the best from Republican and Democratic ideas and put them together" for the good of "the nation as a whole."

Margaret wanted to be known as a candidate, not a woman, but it was hard to escape being defined by her gender. As one of her supporters said, the other candidates were only running for president—Margaret Chase Smith was making history.

What a candidate she was—a truly historic one.

Women in US politics

1872	1925	1933	1964	1972
Victoria Woodhull, first woman to run for president (Equal Rights Party)	Nellie Tayloe Ross of Wyoming, first female governor	Frances Perkins, first female US Cabinet member (Secretary of Labor)	Margaret Chase Smith, first woman from a major political party (Republican) to run for president	Shirley Chisholm, first African American (male or female) to run for president from a major political party (Democratic)

1981
Sandra Day O'Connor, first female justice on the US Supreme Court

1984
Geraldine Ferraro, first female vice presidential nominee from a major political party (Democratic)

1991
Sharon Pratt Dixon, first female African American mayor of a major US city (Washington DC)

1997
Madeleine Albright, first female US Secretary of State

2005
Condoleezza Rice, first female African American Secretary of State

20??
First female US president—who and when?

After losing the presidential nomination, Margaret served in Congress for eight more years until she finally lost her senatorial race in 1972. She lost not because she was a woman, but because some thought she was too old.

She then served as a guest professor at colleges and started the Margaret Chase Smith Library. She had schools and bridges named after her, received ninety-five honorary college degrees, and became one of the first twenty women inducted into the National Women's Hall of Fame. In 1989 President George Herbert Walker Bush presented Margaret with the Presidential Medal of Freedom.

Margaret Chase Smith died at the age of ninety-seven on Memorial Day in 1995. She died at home in her own bed with her purse nearby—her purse, which on that day, as on every other day, contained a copy of the Constitution.

What an American she was—patriotic until the end.
What a president we would have had in … Margaret Chase Smith.

More About Margaret Chase Smith

Born on December 14, 1897, in Skowhegan, Maine (a town of about five thousand people), Margaret was the oldest of six children. She was close to her father, George Chase, until her three brothers were born. Then George seemed to spend more time with the boys. Margaret was close to her mother, Carrie Murray Chase, until the day she died at the age of seventy-seven. Margaret declared her mother's death to be "the greatest sorrow, grief, and tragedy of my life."

Margaret's first childhood friend was the family babysitter, an eleven-year-old girl named Agnes Lamore. Agnes worked six days a week, arriving by 7:00 a.m. to prepare breakfast and not leaving until 8:00 p.m., after getting the youngest children to sleep. When Agnes arrived in the mornings, Margaret was already up, dressed, and waiting. When Agnes asked Margaret why she rose so early, she emphatically answered, "Because I want to do things!"

The money lesson Margaret learned from her grandfather when he loaned her the money for her senior class trip to Washington DC stayed with her. When Margaret ran for Congress and for president, she sent money back to citizens who mailed it to her, not wanting to be a candidate who appeared to owe favors to her contributors. She refused to buy campaign commercials and did not hire workers for her campaigns. In fact, she bragged

The life of Margaret Chase Smith

1897
Born in Skowhegan, Maine, on December 14

1903
Her brother Roland dies of pneumonia

1906
Her brother Lawrence dies of dysentery

1916
Leaves Maine for the first time on her senior class trip to Washington DC; graduates from high school

1922
Organizes Skowhegan chapter of Business and Professional Women

1924
Leaves Maine for the second time to attend the national Business and Professional Women convention in Indiana

that for the Republican presidential primary in Illinois (in which she received 250,000 votes, or thirty percent of the vote) she only spent eighty-five dollars on her campaign.

As a teenager Margaret was interested in practical, hands-on subjects as opposed to academics. In fact, Margaret flunked history in high school—surprising for a woman who would later make history many times over. She started working part-time at the age of thirteen in the local five-and-dime store. Her favorite job, which she had while she was in high school, was as a substitute telephone operator on the night shift. Because there were few calls at night, there was an old couch to sleep on in the telephone office, but Margaret preferred to chat with her friends, talk with operators all over the state, and listen in on others' conversations to learn "everything that went on in town." Margaret first began talking with her future husband, Clyde, when he would call to get the time.

In high school Margaret's favorite activity was basketball. She was the team manager as well as a player; her team won the state championship her senior year. A part of Margaret thrived on being in the center of action.

Margaret and Clyde married on May 14, 1930. It was a small wedding because it was Clyde's second marriage. The reception was another story. Clyde lived in a thirty-two-room mansion, which was filled with three hundred guests from all over the state on their wedding evening.

In 1936, when Clyde was elected to the US House of Representatives, Margaret was excited to move to Washington. Surprisingly, Clyde didn't like Washington. He was anxious to return to Maine and run for

1930	1936	1940	1943	1948	1950
Marries Clyde H. Smith on May 14	Clyde elected as US congressman; the couple moves to Washington DC	Clyde dies; Margaret wins election to take over his seat in House of Representatives	Becomes member of Naval Affairs Committee	Wins election to US Senate, becoming first woman in US history to be elected to both houses of Congress; Women's Armed Services Integration Act becomes a law	Gives "Declaration of Conscience" speech

governor. He died before he got that chance. Margaret had always kept a detailed diary, but her entry that day simply said, "Clyde gone, 12:30 am."

As a short (5 ft. 3 in.), white-haired lady, Margaret was often underestimated in Congress. Her opponents wondered how in the world they'd lost an election, an issue, or a debate to her. Yet Margaret was tough. One morning while campaigning for reelection, she slipped on ice and broke her arm. A few hours later she gave a speech in the next town on the campaign tour, after stopping quickly at the hospital to get her arm set in a cast.

Margaret chose her causes carefully in Congress. Coming from a state with a prominent naval shipyard and air base, it was natural for her to serve on the Naval Affairs Committee and the Armed Services Committee. She believed military readiness and strength were the keys to keeping America safe.

Some wondered why Margaret, with no college education, was such a leader in the development of the space program. She explained, "In my mind, the most significant achievement directly attributed to space exploration is that it has, in so short a time, challenged and stimulated our youth at all educational levels in the quest for scientific knowledge."

Right before Margaret gave her "Declaration of Conscience" speech against Senator Joseph McCarthy, he asked her if she was "going to make a speech." She said that she was and that he would not like it. Many considered her speech to be political suicide. Before her speech, there was much speculation about her being a serious vice presidential candidate. After her speech, Republicans

1954	1955	1957	1959	1964	1968
Becomes member of Senate Armed Services Committee	Introduces her first Rose Resolution, which proposes the rose as the national flower	Flies in a jet and breaks the sound barrier	Becomes member of Aeronautical and Space Sciences Committee	Announces that she will run for the US presidency	Ends her 13-year consecutive roll-call voting record when she has hip surgery

treated her as an outcast for several years. President Dwight Eisenhower said that "he would be happy to have his picture taken with every Republican senator but that Smith woman."

As the first woman from a major political party to run for president, Margaret was honest about her intention to pioneer "the way for a woman in the future . . . to make the way easier for her to be elected president." Even though Margaret knew she would not win, she didn't want to miss seeing her name placed in nomination for the presidency. Candidates were traditionally absent during the speech nominating them. But Margaret eagerly watched as her friend, Vermont senator George Aiken, nominated her as "one of the most capable persons I have ever known." The band played a tribute to Maine, delegates cheered and waved Smith signs, and it was reported that even people watching on TV "smiled through their tears" as they watched history in the making.

Perhaps the object that best symbolized Margaret was the rose. Margaret wore a fresh rose corsage every day throughout her career in Congress. When President John F. Kennedy was assassinated, she removed her rose and silently placed it on the desk where he'd sat as a senator. Margaret presented her first rose resolution, which proposed the rose as the national flower, in 1955 and submitted it year after year. In 1986 President Ronald Reagan finally signed a bill making the rose the national flower. Margaret, just like rose petals, always demonstrated uncommon grace, poise, and beauty. Margaret, just like thorny rose stems, also showed incredible strength, vigor, and toughness.

1972
Loses senate race and is out of office for the first time in 32 years

1973
Inducted into National Women's Hall of Fame

1982
Dedicates Margaret Chase Smith Library

1986
The rose becomes the national flower

1989
Receives Presidential Medal of Freedom

1995
Dies at her home in Skowhegan, Maine, on Memorial Day, May 29

Internet

Margaret Chase Smith Library

http://www.mcslibrary.org Features Margaret Chase Smith's biography, a time line of her life, numerous photos, and an audio recording of "Leave It to the Girls," a song written for the 1964 presidential campaign.

Women in Congress

http://womenincongress.house.gov/profiles Presents biographical information for past and current female members of Congress, essays, and historical images.

Books

Gould, Alberta. *First Lady of the Senate: A Life of Margaret Chase Smith*. Mt. Desert, ME: Windswept House Publishers, 1990.

Mrs. Driver's 1993–94 Fourth-Grade Class at Woolwich Central School. *Highlights of Margaret Chase Smith's Life*. Brunswick, ME: Biddle Publishing Co., 1994.

Northwood University Margaret Chase Smith Library, comp. *Never Underestimate . . . The Life and Career of Margaret Chase Smith Through the Eyes of the Political Cartoonist*. Skowhegan, ME: Northwood University Margaret Chase Smith Library, 1993.

Northwood University Margaret Chase Smith Library, comp. *A Woman for All Seasons: A Photographic Chronicle of Margaret Chase Smith's Career*. Skowhegan, ME: Northwood University Margaret Chase Smith Library, 1992.

Schmidt, Patricia L. *Margaret Chase Smith: Beyond Convention*. Orono, ME: University of Maine Press, 1996.

Sherman, Janann. *No Place for a Woman: A Life of Senator Margaret Chase Smith*. New Brunswick, NJ: Rutgers University Press, 2000.

Sleeper, Frank H. *Margaret Chase Smith's Skowhegan* (Images of America series). Dover, NH: Arcadia Publishing, 1996.

Smith, Margaret Chase. *Declaration of Conscience*. Garden City, NY: Doubleday & Co., 1972.

Multimedia

Wiggins, Patsy and Northwood University Margaret Chase Smith Library. *Margaret Chase Smith: The Voice of Maine, The Conscience of the Senate*. VHS. Orr's Island, Maine: Steve Phillips Video Productions, 1996.

To Visit

Margaret Chase Smith Gallery

Pictures of Margaret Chase Smith are displayed in the visitor center of the Good Will-Hinckley School in Hinckley, Maine. The center is a replica of the homestead of Margaret's grandfather, George Emery Chase.

Margaret Chase Smith Library

Located in Skowhegan, Maine, the library contains political papers, photos and memorabilia (including the orange jumpsuit she wore while breaking the sound barrier), a collection of elephant statues, gifts from world leaders, and a giant time line of Margaret Chase Smith's life and career. A guided tour of Margaret Chase Smith's residence is available by appointment.